GROUNDED IN GOD:

LISTENING HEARTS DISCERNMENT FOR GROUP DELIBERATIONS

Grounded

MOREHOUSE PUBLISHING
Harrisburg, Pennsylvania

Suzanne G. Farnham
Stephanie A. Hull
R. Taylor McLean

In God:

Listening Hearts Discernment for Group Deliberations

Revised Edition

Unless otherwise noted, all Scripture quotations in this book are from
the New Revised Standard Version of the Bible, copyright © 1989
by the Division of Christian Education of the National Council of
the Churches of Christ in the USA. Used by permission. All rights
reserved.

Morehouse Publishing, 4785 Linglestown Road, Suite 101 Harrisburg, Pa. 17112

Morehouse Publishing, 19 East 34th Street, New York, NY 10016

Morehouse Publishing is an imprint of Church Publishing Incorporated

Library of Congress Cataloging-in-Publication Data
Farnham, Suzanne G.
      Grounded in God : listening hearts discernment for group
deliberations / Suzanne G. Farnham, Stephanie A. Hull, R. Taylor
McLean.
           p. cm.
      Includes bibliographical references.
      ISBN 13 : 978-0-8192-1835-3
      1. Church group work. 2. Discernment of spirits. I. Hull,
Stephanie A. II. McLean, R. Taylor. III. Title
BV652.2.F37   1996
253.7—dc20   96-18840   CIP

Printed in the United States of America

10 10 9

Contents

Acknowledgments

Three of us wrote this book together in prayerful community, but not without substantial help from a constellation of people.

First and foremost, we thank Marilynn E. Cornejo and John E. McIntyre. Efficiently and in good humor, Marilynn typed countless drafts of our work as it progressed and developed over many months. John then combined his mastery of the English language and his solid background in theology to edit the copy for us.

We appreciate the contribution of +A. Theodore Eastman, Sarah T. Eastman, and W. Bruce McPherson+, who joined us in the research. Four other people were particularly helpful as we gathered information and processed it. Arthur Larrabee and Nancy Middleton, Clerk and General Secretary, respectively, of the Philadelphia Yearly Meeting, met with a group of us for several hours; Arthur also gave us a highly informative set of notes he has assembled for a book. Jan Hoffman, who is active in the New England Yearly Meeting and lectures on Quaker subjects in this country and abroad, has graciously supplied us with relevant published materials and served as a mentor for several years. Michael Sheeran, S. J., President of Regis College in Denver and author of *Beyond Majority Rule*, helped with the wording of several endnotes.

William Rich+ and Jeannine Ruof gave generously of their time and skill to help solve difficulties with gender-inclusive language in the Introduction.

When we completed a draft of the first few chapters, Joseph Booze, Adele B. Free, Linda Wofford Hawkins+, and Benjamin West reviewed it and offered suggestions. After the preliminary draft was completed, a number of friends and colleagues read the entire manuscript and offered thoughtful comments that enabled us to improve the work in significant ways: Mary De Kuyper, Wayne Dornbirer II, James C. Fenhagen+, Bliss and Lois Forbush, Miriam D. Green, Linda Wofford Hawkins+, Jan Hoffman, Martha Horton, +Robert Ihloff, W. Bruce McPherson+, Shirley Noll, and Susan M. Ward.

Frank Shivers, author and English professor, was available for consultation whenever asked. Others provided a wide range of support throughout: Lyman (Barney) Farnham+, Pauline Fredritz, Adele B. Free, Louise E. Miller, and Maureen O'Ferrall.

We thank our editor, Deborah Grahame-Smith, who not

only was readily available to us, but also suggested the title *Grounded in God*—which we all hailed without hesitation.

We are ever grateful to Memorial Episcopal Church in Baltimore for office space and steadfast support at all levels.

And finally, we appreciate the personal support and sacrifice of those close to us, especially Anne Blumenberg, Barney Farnham+, Samuel King, and Peggy M. McLean.

Thanks be to God for blessing us so richly.

Background
of this Book

Grounded in God: Listening Hearts Discernment for Group Deliberations builds on a foundation built by a network of people under the auspices of the Christian Vocation Project–also known as Listening Hearts Ministries–who have developed programs, published materials, and provided training to encourage and enable the practice of spiritual discernment in the church. Their initial book *Listening Hearts: Discerning Call in Community* draws upon the spiritual classics and experience from a wide range of Christian traditions to explore the themes of call, discernment, and community as they relate to each other; this seminal work seeks to help the church become more a community of support for individuals as they wrestle with issues, relationships, priorities, and life-choices. Three companion pieces provide program resources to accompany the book:

Listening Hearts Manual for Discussion Leaders, Listening Hearts Retreat Designs and Meditation Exercises, and the *Listening Hearts Songbook.* Now *Grounded in God* is offered to help move the community of faith forward to practice spiritual discernment while making group decisions and tending to the affairs of the church.

Introduction

*Spiritual discernment is a prayerful, informed, and
intentional effort to distinguish God's voice
from other voices that influence us.*

Thy will be done on earth. Jesus gave these words to
the disciples, and his followers have been praying
them ever since. Spiritual discernment is the quest to
discover God's will for us so that we can live into
these words of the Lord's Prayer and all that they
imply. Discernment was central in the life of Jesus,
who came into the world to do the work of God.
Jesus expressed it this way: "I can do nothing on my
own... I seek to do not my own will but the will of
[the one] who sent me" (Jn. 5:30). Doing God's work
provided Jesus' very sustenance: "Doing the will of the

one who sent me and bringing this work to comple-
tion is my food" (Jn. 4:34 INT).

Jesus did not act alone but remained in close personal
contact with God: "...I do nothing on my own, but I
speak these things as [God] instructed me. And the
one who sent me is with me; [and] has not left me
alone...." (Jn. 8:28-29).

Jesus directed his followers to continue God's work in
the world: "As you have sent me into the world, so I
have sent them into the world" (Jn. 17:18), and "You
did not choose me but I chose you. And I appointed
you to go and bear fruit, fruit that will last...." (Jn.
15:16).

Jesus warned his followers that they would be unable
to do God's work without the closest mutual
indwelling: "I am the vine, you are the branches.
Those who abide in me and I in them bear much fruit,
because apart from me you can do nothing" (Jn. 15:5).

Jesus then promised to impart the Holy Spirit to us
and to remain with us always: "...the Holy Spirit,
whom [God] will send in my name, will teach you
everything..." (Jn. 14:26), and "And remember, I am
with you always, to the end of the age" (Mt. 28:20).

Just hours before he was crucified, Jesus prayed that those who were to follow his first disciples might all be one: "...as you, [God], are in me and I am in you, may they also be in us...." (Jn. 17:21).

We are the body of Christ in today's world. It is thus both our call and our fulfillment to permit God to act in us and through us as we do business as the church. This book has been written to provide a resource for church groups that would like to approach their deliberations in the spirit of discernment. The authors have been working with various church bodies over the past several years, developing ways to make the practice of spiritual discernment a widespread reality. They hope that this book will provide insight and inspiration to people active in the affairs of the church. In this way the people of God can both enact their faith and deepen their love and trust[1] while working out community decisions that they face as the body of Christ. The Appendices offer practical suggestions for those who want to implement the ideas discussed in this book.

Let the Lord your God show us where we should go and what we should do. –Jer. 42:3

Spiritual Discernment: Its Meaning and Value for Group Meetings

When the day of Pentecost had come, they were all together in one place. And suddenly from heaven there came a sound like the rush of a violent wind, and it filled the entire house where they were sitting. —Acts 2:1-2

Imagine a church on a breezy spring day, its doors and windows opened wide to let the wind flow through. So it is when we come together as God's people with the doors of our hearts and minds open— our eyes as windows raised to see what God will show us, our ears open to hear what God may say. It is then that the wind of the Spirit can sweep into our midst to make Pentecost a reality in our life together.

God knows our deepest potential, sees the hidden complexities of our circumstances, comprehends our situation in relation to the larger picture, and grasps the broader implications of our plans. Discernment[1] is our effort to tap into the flow of this divine wisdom.

In classical spirituality, discernment means distinguishing God's Spirit from other spirits that are present in a given time and place—such as the spirit of a nation, the spirit of the times, the spirit of competition. To put it another way, discernment is distinguishing the voice of God from other voices that speak to us: the voice of our parents echoing from years past, the voices of friends, voices of urgency or fear. These voices are neither bad nor good in and of themselves. God often speaks to us through them. But, if followed indiscriminantly, such voices can dominate us and lead us along a wrong path.

Discernment is a prayerful, informed, and intentional attempt to sort through these voices to get in touch with God's Spirit at work in a situation and to develop a sense of the direction in which the Spirit is leading. Discernment is more a journey than a destination. We may not find answers for all our concerns, but we can be receptive to God's presence as we ponder the questions.[2]

Sound rational analysis based on the best available information is crucial to good discernment. Yet spiritual discernment goes beyond the analytical to engage our senses, feelings, imaginations, and intuition as we wrestle with issues. It often points toward a decision, but it is **not** problem-solving. The goal of our discernment efforts is to find the mind of Christ.[3] As such, it is the central component of decision-making for those who would have their lives grounded in God.

Discernment is more than saying prayers that ask God to guide us in rational consideration of matters. It is a mode of prayer that involves opening our entire selves to the working of the Holy Spirit. It bids us to let go of preconceived ideas so that we can be open to new possibilities with a readiness to view things from new perspectives. Discernment beckons us to be still and listen with the ear of our heart. It draws us into alignment with God.

Discernment is central to doing God's work. To serve God, we must constantly be alert to the presence and guidance of the Holy Spirit. Without God, we can do nothing. "Those who abide in me and I in them," said Jesus, "bear much fruit, because apart from me you can do nothing" (Jn. 15:5).

In group deliberations, discernment involves coming together with open hearts and open minds to seek God's wisdom around issues important to the community. The first order of business is to become attuned to God's presence within and among those assembled.

Groups that seek discernment when they have business to do and decisions to make often find that their meetings become more energized and productive. The priorities of the meeting shift. Those gathered grow in faith and in love for one another while addressing the issues at hand. When those present center in God and listen deeply, their varying needs and divergent views can move from discord to concord. Rather than entering into a contest with factions singing competing tunes, the group as a whole can discover a true harmony, satisfying for all.

Spiritual discernment differs from other kinds of discernment because it is grounded in a conviction that the Holy Spirit is an active presence and, when in a group, the leading party in the proceedings. Christ is present at the center of each person and alive in the group—speaking, forming, and touching—waiting to be heard and recognized. Those assembled want to let go of barriers, both individually and collectively. They want the Spirit to guide them in shaping an issue so that it reflects what is important to God. The Spirit works as leaven that permeates the mixture, transforming the ingredients into the bread of life.

Issues of seemingly great import can become insignificant when measured against our relationship with God. For example, when a man asked Jesus to tell his brother to divide the family inheritance with him, Jesus shifted the perspective to the problem of greed, pointing out that one's life does not consist in the abundance of one's possessions. He then told a parable that warned against storing up treasures for oneself without being rich toward God (Luke 12:13). Engaging Jesus in dialogue moved the discussion from a perfectly logical consideration of property rights to the importance of putting our relationship with God first. Such reordering of priorities enables a group to be more useful in the Lord's service.

The kingdom of heaven is like yeast that a woman took and mixed in with three measures of flour until all of it was leavened. —Mt. 13:33

TWO

Total Listening

A spirit glided past my face; the hair of my flesh bristled.
It stood still, but I could not discern its appearance.
A form was before my eyes; there was silence,
then I heard a voice.... – Job 4:15-16

Focused silence creates a stillness in which particular sounds become distinctly heard or felt. It is as though a veil is lifted from our senses and intuitions. We see our brothers and sisters anew; we hear afresh the sounds in the silence. We feel the Spirit in our midst.

In contrast, if the noise level is loud enough, it may be impossible to hear people talking to us, even if they shout. That is how it sometimes is with God: God is speaking to us, but the noise around us is so great that we hear nothing. If a group wants to hear God, the first thing its members must do is to create a serene environment.

Beyond that, we contend with inner commotion. Many voices chatter inside us as we think about what we had been doing before we arrived and worry about what we have yet to do after we leave. Our muscles may be tense, our bodies full of stress. To listen to God, we need to become still within. We need to become quiet as a group. Beginning meetings in silence provides an opportunity for a group to settle down and become attuned to God's presence.[1]

Once a quiet tone is established, it is important to maintain it by proceeding in ways that encourage genuine listening. For instance, if the group takes care to allow a pause between speakers, it provides time for everyone to absorb what has been said.[2] Moreover, the speaker may have a deeper thought percolating underneath and will find that a pause opens an opportunity to discover and articulate a new insight. By honoring the pause, we avoid interrupting the speaker without careful consideration. In those silent pauses, we leave time for God to mold us gently before we move on.

A more subtle problem is our tendency to formulate what we want to say next while another person is speaking. We cannot truly listen if we are focused on what we ourselves want to say. Discernment is not an exercise in persuasion; rather, it is an attempt to listen deeply and await God's guidance.[3]

Attentive listening goes beyond the spoken word. In discernment, we listen with our eyes as well as with our ears, observing facial expressions and body language. People tell us many things by how they are sitting, how they are holding their heads, what they are doing with their hands, or by the expressions on their faces.

In addition, we need to listen with our feelings. Whatever emotions are stimulated within us at a meeting are telling us something—perhaps about ourselves, perhaps about what is being said, maybe about both. Times of quiet make it possible to hold emotional reactions in prayer and await guidance. The group as a whole can be invited to sit before God with its feelings. Meetings in which honest, quiet prayer and sharing are the norm knit people together in Christ.

Our intuition and imagination are other vehicles for listening. If the tone and pace of the gathering are sufficiently reflective, pictures may emerge in our imagination or passages of Scripture may come to mind. These may provide more insight than thousands of words. A vivid image can be shared with the group and explored for meaning.

Finally, we need to listen to the group as a whole as well as to the individuals within it. Are there things not being said, questions not being raised? If so, why? Is anyone dominating the group? Are some people not getting an adequate opportunity to speak? Are people truly engaged, whether they are speaking or not? Is there a prayerful sense of God's presence?

If listening is cultivated as a habit in all aspects of life, the continuity between our daily lives and the occasions of our meetings will grow and develop, each enriching the other.[4] God speaks through people, through events, and through the circumstances of our lives. Most especially, God speaks through the community gathered in the spirit of prayerful listening. Groups that nurture the practice of reverent listening in their lives apart as well as in their times together grow closer to one another as they grow closer to God.

Listen to me in silence, O coastlands; Let the peoples renew their strength; let them approach, then let them speak; let us together draw near for judgment.
—Isa. 41:1

THREE

Searching for Questions Before Answers

*If one gives answer before hearing,
it is folly and shame.* —Prov. 18:13

Peter, James, and John were alone on the mountain with
Jesus. They had just seen Jesus transfigured, flanked by
Moses and Elijah. Not knowing what to say, Peter blurted
out, "Rabbi, it is good for us to be here; let us make
three dwellings, one for you, one for Moses, and one for
Elijah" (Mk. 9:5). His response to an experience of awe
was to call for action, something tangible and doable.

We live in an action-oriented society. Our response to
uncertainty or confusion is to begin offering solutions.
Like Peter, when exposed to something startling or
inexplicable, our reflex is to explain and contain the
phenomenon. Often in a meeting, a question or problem

is no sooner stated than a barrage of remedies begins—"Have you tried this or that?" "Why don't we do such and such?" "Well, what we need is a system to...." "The way I see this issue is...."

Resting in uncertainty goes against the grain, especially in a business meeting. Groups rush to solutions. They feel the pressure of time. They believe that quick action is expected of them and that it demonstrates efficiency. Fear and anxiety may prompt a group to clamp a lid on difficult questions. To explore an issue may be painful, force a change, or delay action; but it can also be a doorway to greater understanding. It is not that solutions are undesirable; rather, an early solution may shut off a deeper exploration of the question and foreclose the opportunity to listen to God and one another.

A question in and of itself does not necessarily tell us what level of response is appropriate. For example, "Where are we meeting?" may be a simple request for information. On the other hand, it may reflect problems with the meeting place—perhaps it is too distant, someone else's territory, inaccessible or inconvenient for some. If we raise and consider questions carefully, we may detect an unstated need that may be important to address. One person's concern often turns out to be shared by others. Responding to an individual's concern gives people in the group an opportunity to care for one another and build community.

When considered seriously, a question often changes with time and reflection. As the question becomes clear and focused, the answer may reveal itself. It is important to provide opportunity for people first to ask questions that establish the needed information, and then to allow time to raise questions that get beneath the surface, revealing the signs of God's presence in the situation: "...members of a community intent on discernment must be deeply united to Christ, not only to find an answer to their problem, but to ask the right question in the first place."[1] Group meetings are dynamic. Time and uncertainty, often seen as enemies, can become allies in shaping the unknown and in resolving issues—sometimes without our even doing anything explicit to work them out.

To illustrate this last thought: One group was in sharp disagreement on a matter and decided to spend a Saturday morning together in discernment. They did so; and at the end of three hours, people felt agitated, their divisions appeared even stronger, and the situation felt hopeless. Nonetheless, they agreed to continue to pray and to come back together for another

Saturday morning of discernment. On this second Saturday, the tone was entirely different. A powerful sense of God's presence enveloped the meeting. As people listened and spoke with reverence, the group found itself viewing the questions before them in a new way. In the course of the morning they came into clear spiritual consensus, which left them grateful that they had persisted in prayer and waiting–and marveling at the way God works through people who come together with listening hearts.

Moreover, creative exchanges can shift our focus. One day Jesus and his disciples were pestered by a Canaanite woman begging Jesus to heal her daughter. Jesus ignored the woman, and the disciples urged him to send her away. Jesus said to the woman, "I was sent only to the lost sheep of the house of Israel." She persisted and knelt before him saying, "Lord, help me." He answered, "It is not fair to take the children's food and throw it to the dogs." She answered, "Yes, Lord, yet even the dogs eat the crumbs that fall from their masters' table." At this, Jesus exclaimed, "Woman, great is your faith! Let it be done for you as you wish." Her daughter was healed instantly (Mt. 15:24-28). The willingness of Jesus and the woman to be open to each other released the power that healed the little girl.[2]

Probing questions engage us in ways that help us to discover things for ourselves so that they become our own and bear authority for us. Answers provided by others seldom carry the same weight. Good questions can open us up to the creative flow of the Spirit. Well-framed questions can draw the entire group into a search for truth that enables its members to develop fuller insight together. Then answers and actions may follow more serviceably.

> *"Hear and I will speak; I will question you, and you declare to me." I had heard of you by the hearing of the ear, but now my eye sees you....*
> *–Job 42:4-6*

FOUR

Engaging the Imagination

Then the angel showed me the river of the water of life,
bright as crystal.... –Rev. 22:1a

He was an artistic man–creative, with significant professional accomplishment. But his troubled life moved from crisis to crisis. He often cried out for help. Over the years, a number of people from the local church community went to great lengths to help him out. Without fail, he would push them beyond their limits, demanding more than they could give. Eventually the inevitable breach would fracture another relationship.

A woman from the congregation was in a deep silence, holding this man in prayer, when a vivid picture flooded her imagination: an enormous thistle, glorious with purple bloom, appeared in the window.

It was so real that she checked to see if it was physically there. Through this unanticipated image, God provided insight that could be shared with those concerned. A blossoming thistle is a plant of beauty. Butterflies—symbolic of the Resurrection—feed on the nectar of its flower. Yet beware of getting too close! Thistles do not allow people to touch them. This mental picture helped the people involved realize that they could not touch this man's life directly as they had been trying. But perhaps they could touch him in some other way by recognizing his inner beauty and the potential of his work.

Sometimes a common image arises. During a retreat for a board of directors of a church conference center, the members reflected on the board's role in relationship to the church. As reflections were shared, a number of people began to express images of water—moving water that turned over and renewed itself, water that moved outward like the concentric waves created by a pebble dropped into a lake. This water image helped members of the board recognize an historical problem that had plagued the staff and leadership. The rural location of the facility and its distance from the center of church activities in the state, both literally and figuratively, often created a sense of isolation and separateness. The board and staff often spoke of "them and us." The water images helped the board see its role as always moving out, reshaping and extending its ministry. These images continued to come up in discussions as the board worked to renew the conference center and its relationships.

Facts, figures, and objective data are crucial to making responsible decisions. But other factors influence the flow of events as well: unconscious fears, unarticulated hopes, hidden passions, subtle relationships. Much of reality is invisible and intangible. Those who consider concrete information alone limit their vision.

Throughout the Bible and throughout the history of the church, God has spoken to people through dreams and visions. A vision is a kind of spontaneous image—a dream that occurs while awake. We live in a scientific culture that emphasizes observed empirical data, one that can benefit from the use of our creative faculties to arrive at new insight through images and dreams. And so, as we go about business, decision-making and goal-setting, we do well to permit imagination and images to break in and inform us.

The Bible abounds with accounts of visions through which God guided the people of Israel. At times a vision was given to one person for the benefit of many. For example, Pharaoh's two dreams—interpreted by Joseph—helped great numbers of people to prepare for a severe famine (Gen. 41:1-36).

At other times an image was shared by the leaders of a community or by the community as a whole. Such was the case in the wilderness as the Hebrews journeyed toward the promised land: "The Lord went in front of them in a pillar of cloud by day, to lead them along the way, and in a pillar of fire by night, to give them light, so they might travel by day and by night. Neither the pillar of cloud by day nor the pillar of fire by night left its place in front of the people" (Ex. 13:21-22).

The more members of a group are familiar with the Bible[1], the more readily God can speak through it to those assembled. When considering an issue, a person or group may feel magnetically drawn to a particular passage. This may indicate that God has something to say about the situation through it. If those meeting take time to reflect on that portion of Scripture, they may develop considerable clarity.

God speaks through art and music as well. Sometimes as we struggle with a question or find ourselves caught up in the heat of a meeting, a melody or song skips across our mind, or we see flashes of a painting, or we start to think of a scene from a play or movie. We may feel the movement of dance in our bodies. Such experiences emerge spontaneously and can provide insight into questions or bring comfort and release to a difficult moment if we allow them to rise in our consciousness. For example, during an agitated church budget meeting, a woman began to hear the chant "Be Still and Know That I Am God"[2] echo through her mind. This moved her to ask for a slower, more prayer-centered pace.[3] The deliberations became more thoughtful, the tone more caring. Though the work was difficult, the group completed it with a sense of unity.

When people gather intent upon centering in God and listening to one another, they fashion an atmosphere of hospitality to the Spirit. The potential for being touched by God's truth and wisdom is heightened. In the company of the Spirit, the potential of the group far exceeds what the individuals together bring to it. The likelihood that spontaneous images will arise increases. Such images can be visual, auditory, or intuitive. They come not from the head but emerge from the depths with great strength. They tend to have an indelible quality. They are symbolic and, when explored for meaning, often bear a clear message.

Human beings have been endowed with enormous gifts of creativity and imagination, gifts to be welcomed as pathways from God to us, and from us to God.[4] In groups, the images of one person can stimulate the thoughts and images of others. Imagination helps God break through to us in ways that go beyond our customary modes of analysis, discussion, and rational thought. Just as God called Moses when he turned aside to see the burning bush, so, too, may God speak to us when we turn aside and attend to where the Spirit may be leading. By paying attention to all of our senses and the flow of our imaginations, we may be emancipated from our various preconceptions. We become open for God to carry us beyond the limits of our personal knowledge and ability to analyze.[5]

Then the mystery was revealed to Daniel in a vision of the night, and Daniel blessed the God of heaven. —Dan. 2:19

FIVE

Catching the Signals

"Pay attention, come to me;
listen and your soul will live." —Isa. 55:3 JB

If the radio station is transmitting signals but our
radio is not turned on and tuned in, we hear nothing.
Moreover, we have to be near the radio and paying
attention to actually hear what the broadcast is about.
Seeking God through discernment is like tuning in:
God may be sending us signals, but unless our hearts
are prepared, we do not hear. The first step in discernment is to listen, to be attentive.

Next we need to tune into the right station. Filtering
out the other voices that fill the airwaves can help us
find God's message. To do this, we have to know some
of the signs that God uses and how to interpret them.

God's peace is the pre-eminent sign: a sense of confidence at a very deep level indicates that we are moving in the right direction. As a group considers an issue, the members will feel permeated with this peace as they approach God's perspective on the matter before them. On the contrary, they will feel agitated if competing voices confuse them. Yet God's peace does not suggest an absence of struggle. Pretending to agree and be in harmony can create an illusion of peace, but such apparent consonance is weak and superficial.[1] The peace of God is born of bold searching, honest expression, mutual respect, and genuine compassion. Turbulence and turmoil are likely, especially in the initial stages. But ultimately the power of God's truth and love brings serenity and a sense of well-being.[2]

Another way God indicates the presence of the Spirit is through **joy**, sometimes even a feeling of elation. On occasion, this joy carries with it a great surge of **energy** that brings momentum to the group and helps move it into action.

Persistence is another sign. When the same message keeps coming to a group from different places and in various ways, it may be God trying to get through. When this happens, take notice!

Still another way that God's hand shows itself is through **convergence**. Various things that the group has been thinking about and doing over a period of time—things that had seemed unrelated—suddenly come together and make sense. Or the skills and resources of a group may uniquely fit together with a particular need that comes to the fore. Or a special combination of challenges and opportunities presents itself unsolicited.

Finally, God sometimes encourages us through **fruit-fulness**. Ezekiel proclaimed that along the river issuing forth from the temple "will grow every kind of fruit tree with leaves that never wither and fruit that never fails..." (Ez. 47:12, JB). When certain endeavors produce abundant fruit, God may be calling us to cultivate those areas further. But do not declare a tree barren too hastily. In the parable of the fig tree, the owner of the vineyard wanted to cut down the tree because it had been there for three years without producing fruit. The man who looked after the vineyard replied, "Sir, leave it one year and give me time to dig around it and manure it: it may bear fruit next year; if not, then you can cut it down" (Lk. 13:6-9, JB).

We can never be certain that we are hearing God correctly. It is unlikely that all the signs will be present in any given circumstance. We interpret signals as ably as we can, and move forward to act on what we believe God is asking of us, always listening and asking God to continue to guide us and let us know if our understanding is faulty. Discernment is subject to human limitations.[3] We cannot endure the full intensity of God's light. Sometimes we need to grow in small spurts. "[God's] pedagogy throughout the time of the Old and New Covenants has been to introduce his people step by step into the fullness of truth and love".[4]

Our discernment is never complete. As we act on what we understand, God continues to point the way further. Groups need to be alert for signs such as peace, joy, energy, persistence, converging strands, and fruitfulness in relation to their work.[5]

> *"If only you had been alert to my commandments,*
> *your happiness would have been like a river...."*
> *—Isa. 48:18, JB*

Spiritual Consensus: A Way of Coming Together in Christ

How very good and pleasant it is when kindred live together in unity! It is like the precious oil on the head, running down upon the beard, on the beard of Aaron, running down over the collar of his robes. —Ps. 133:1-2

The process of making group decisions can either divide those involved into factions or can knit them together into a strong community. The practice of majority rule that dominates our culture tends to create winners and losers. A majority can easily gloss over the concerns of a minority even when the minority loses only by a vote or two. Sometimes those who exert the most pressure are the ones who prevail. The people on the losing side may feel ignored, beaten, alienated. The feelings and contributions of minorities are often discounted and soon forgotten by those who carry the day.

Another approach to making community decisions is consensus, which creates neither winners nor losers. Consensus literally means "perceiving together." A group that seeks consensus avoids taking votes[1] and instead searches for solutions that satisfy the group as a whole. Anyone in the group who feels strongly can stand firm and block consensus.[2] But consensus does not mean unanimity;[3] rather, it suggests that a sense of the group exists and that everyone feels sufficiently heard to be able to go along with the emerging sentiment. It is important that people who have concerns articulate them clearly to the others. However, if no one else comes to share those concerns, they may need to be explained in some other way. Or perhaps they need to be dropped, at least for the time being.[4]

At times, a group may not come to consensus on a given matter. The time may not be ripe. In such situations, the consensus of the group may be that more time and prayer are needed. Such lack of resolution is part of human experience. Rather than being viewed as failure, it can be seen as a point on the path toward clarity and communion with one another and with God. Consensus often unfolds over time and may not fit into a predesigned schedule. Allowing the Spirit freedom to work in the group is more important than reaching a definitive outcome at a particular time.

For consensus to succeed, every member must remain ever open to seeing things in new ways. Everyone needs to listen and look for ways to bring things together. Consensus requires an atmosphere of mutual respect.

For secular groups and even many church groups, developing consensus is primarily a rational endeavor, achieved through discussion and debate. Spiritual consensus[5] for Christians is a particular approach to consensus. While it, too, draws upon our human skill and talent and makes full use of available data, study and discussion, it goes beyond them to wait upon the Spirit for guidance and direction. In the words of William Temple, what we are looking for is the Spirit's guidance "in its living relationship to the facts confronting it."[6]

It is important that the group cultivate an attitude of humility that flows from a conviction that each of us has limited vision, that even collectively we see but partially, that only God sees everything. Beyond that, those seeking spiritual consensus work under the assumption that God speaks through people, most especially through those gathered in Christ intent upon reverent listening. It is essential that participants be willing to move away from preconceived ideas and personal preferences. Spiritual discernment emerges from a shared desire to discover what God is saying to us together as a community.

Spiritual consensus brings those involved together at a deep level, engendering love and nurturing trust in both God and one another. This may enable a group to develop a position that frees individuals to hold divergent opinions and pursue varying courses of action. When people are bonded together in the Spirit, they develop mutual respect that honors the integrity of each person's point of view. Unity does not require uniformity.[7]

When a group operating under parliamentary procedure considers a controversial proposal, it normally works out a compromise in order to produce a majority vote. While spiritual consensus can produce compromise, more typically those gathered start to see the situation from a new perspective that reveals a path not previously envisioned. Whereas a compromise rarely energizes anyone, a totally new idea that breaks through from God produces enthusiasm (*en theos*, literally "in God").

We cannot achieve spiritual consensus by merely fine-tuning group skills and techniques. Although spiritual consensus takes practice, ultimately it comes as a grace-filled gift from God. Those who await the Spirit as they confront their common concerns can hope to experience the love of God bonding them together in heart and mind.

> *There is one body and one Spirit....*
> *—Eph. 4:4*

SEVEN

Launching Out

Do not be conformed to this world, but be transformed by
the renewal of your minds, so that you may discern what is
the will of God—what is good and acceptable and perfect.
—Rom. 12:2

When church groups gather for business meetings,
they typically follow a secular model derived from
parliamentary procedure. They may begin with prayer,
a meditation, or a time of sharing; they may end with
a prayer. They surely bring Christian principles with
them. But the structure and procedures they use are
essentially indistinguishable from the meetings of
other institutions.

All of our work involves our relationship with God.
The joy and life that flow from being in relationship
with God can be accessible even in the most tedious
and mundane committee work. It is possible for us to

grow in our faith as we resolve budgetary and personnel questions as well as matters of faith and morality. How can a group conducting business as God's people resist conforming to the dominant culture of the secular world? How can a group be constantly transformed and renewed so that they and their work become a living song of praise and love?

Preparation is needed to help a group move toward a new way of doing things. An *ad hoc* group that is working on a limited-term project might not have time to prepare for discernment in a formal way. But one or more elements of discernment, such as prayerful listening and consensus, can be introduced to such a group. Any practice that helps the group become more attuned to the Spirit will strengthen its life and improve the quality of its work.

For example, when a search committee was formed to recommend a new pastor for a large church, the committee chair and several members had had some exposure to discernment principles and practices. After these members spoke to the committee about the value of prayer, silence, and consensus, the group adopted these practices as guidelines for its work. As the work proceeded, some of the members who had initially been unfamiliar with discernment began to take responsibility for calling the committee back to these guidelines. Ultimately, with patience and prayer, the committee achieved spiritual consensus in arriving at its recommendation. This approach not only helped the committee to complete its work, but also enriched the spiritual lives of the members involved.

A long-term group may want to be intentional about developing a new way of working together. Such a group may find it beneficial to prepare in a methodical manner through reading and retreats. Appendix Seven of this book offers suggestions to help a group learn about discernment and prepare to use it as part of decision-making.

Other groups may respond better to a less direct approach, in which case a leader may be able to conduct meetings in such a way that a good bit of discernment unfolds naturally. Over time, participants may notice a change in how they are doing business. Eventually, they may want to learn about discernment in a way that would enable all the members to share in its implementation.

Whatever path a group follows, it can be helpful for everyone to consider these basic tenets:

- The church is the body of Christ in the world today; as such, God has much to accomplish in and through us as we live and work together.

- God is an active and living presence among us as we meet.

- We need to remind ourselves repeatedly that it is the mind of Christ we are seeking in a given situation.

- Insight into how God can best make use of us in a particular circumstance flows from the trust we have in God and the commitment we make to listening for God's guidance on the issues before us.

- We must hold ourselves ready to respond with love and in obedience to what we understand to be God's call.

- Prayer is central to discernment: prayer before we come to meetings, prayer throughout the meetings, prayer by others on behalf of the meetings, prayer after we leave a meeting. Prayer in silence.

> Undefended listening for the leading of
> the Holy Spirit. Teaching the heart to
> watch and wait.

Each person in the group should be encouraged to take responsibility for keeping the group true to the principles of discernment. This will help heighten the awareness of all participants and strengthen the bonds of Christian community. When leadership is shared, people feel empowered and become energized. The more that members feel responsible for the workings of the meeting, the stronger the group becomes.[1]

Once we become discerning members of a group, we are intentional about allowing God to influence our actions. It may be the Spirit's intent that we introduce ideas or suggest actions. Or we may be led simply to listen and pray—waiting to see if God will give us words to articulate. Waiting upon the Spirit, we may become the leaven that helps transform a group into a spiritually discerning body.

There is no sure formula for discerning the mind of God on a particular point. "Communal discernment does not lay the future bare, nor does it take the community to the promised land overnight."[2] But as we respond to God's love with growing trust and gratitude, we experience God's faithfulness and find that God's work is being done through us.

> *But speaking the truth in love, we must grow up in every way into him who is the head, into Christ....* –*Eph. 4:15*

EIGHT

Planning Meetings

...prepare the way of the Lord....
—Isa. 40:3

Envision the business meeting as worship.[1] Think of
the work of the meeting as an expression of our love
for God. Then preparing for meetings becomes holy
work, and developing an agenda becomes the planning of a liturgy. Prepare with reverence for the work
to be done. Think about how the agenda can open the
meeting to God's presence. Most importantly, prepare
with prayer for God's presence and guidance. Brother
Lawrence, a Carmelite monk of the seventeenth century, offers good advice on practicing the presence of
God in what seem to be the most mundane chores.
"The time of business," he said, "does not with me
differ from the time of prayer, and in the noise and

clatter of my kitchen, while several persons are at the same time calling for different things, I possess God in as great tranquility as if I were upon my knees at the Blessed Sacrament."[2]

God is present in our every effort and in each person with whom we work. The keystone for constructing an agenda might be the question, "How can we help prepare a way for God's presence to be felt in our work?" Our approach to a meeting and the meeting itself could then be transformed. The content of the meeting involves business matters; but more deeply the purpose of the meeting is to be present to God in the work.

In our church work we often see boards and committees on which the participants seem tired or undertake business in a perfunctory manner. Yet, many in our churches long for spiritual growth and renewal even as they work on business matters. We can shape agendas that prepare a way to find the Holy Spirit in our meetings.

Plan lean. Spare agendas allow a reflective pace conducive to discernment. Hone the agenda; keep it simple. Reduce a broad issue to two or three questions. Simple agendas help focus meetings.

It is difficult to have reflective deliberations if the agenda is not thoughtfully prepared. Appendix 3 ("Checklist for Preparing an Agenda") provides guidance toward this end.

Boards and committees are most effective if they concentrate on larger policy questions, approaching fewer decisions with greater care. Ideally, a church body will not take on more business than it can manage in a prayer-centered way. Groups may want to consider scheduling fewer, but longer meetings—all day or overnight or longer—so that more reflective, in-depth attention can be given to issues.

A board that concentrates its efforts on the major policy decisions can then keep track of subsidiary decisions to be sure that they are consistent with its policies. It can set up an executive committee of officers or other designated members to make routine decisions. It can also delegate appropriate responsibilities to committees and individuals, giving them authority to carry out the tasks they take on. This means that members actively engage in the work of the group between meetings. When this route is taken, someone must be responsible for coordinating the work to make sure that it gets done.

Good communication is necessary to keep everyone abreast of what others are doing. Those working collaboratively outside of meetings can do so in various ways, such as phone calls, meetings, fax, mail, and interactive computers. People working on related issues can keep one another informed by similar means. Concise written reports can be distributed with the agenda before meetings. Avoid lengthy reports at meetings, but provide opportunities for questions and dialogue about the reports.

Consider integrating traditional aspects of worship such as prayer, Scripture, and song into the meeting. Periods of silence or prayer can occur at any time in the course of a meeting to help people refocus.

Music can set the tone for a meeting. Singing can help center a group as a meeting begins or following a break. Songs can be selected spontaneously to capture the substance of what has transpired and help move the group forward.

The Bible can be a major channel for discernment. One way of drawing upon Scripture is to select a passage that may shed light on a question scheduled for consideration and then plan a discernment meditation exercise as part of the meeting (see Appendix Four).

Or, if members of a group are encouraged to introduce biblical texts or images for reflection spontaneously over the course of the deliberations, the habit of seeking guidance through Scripture can be cultivated.

When someone offers a Scripture reference, be sure to provide opportunity for brainstorming, silence, and sharing reflections. It is crucial not to use Scripture to manipulate a group. Using Scripture to establish a point or justify an argument is quite different from being open to the Spirit's guidance through Scripture.

Unless a reflective pace is maintained in the meeting, there will be little opportunity for Scripture to surface. If a Scripture passage is suggested at a meeting, but there is not adequate time to reflect on it, it can be designated as a meditation text for the next meeting.

Finally, do not forget the human side. People need time and opportunity to get to know one another. They need to address issues of trust, reflect on the dynamics within the group, and acknowledge individual contributions and group achievements. These elements can be built into the meeting, provided for as a prelude or postlude to a meeting, or planned as separate events. For instance, gathering for a meal before a meeting can provide an occasion to celebrate a special accomplishment.

In planning meetings, tend to the needs of the group and design agendas that help participants to be centered in God's presence. Integrating the love of God with the business at hand follows in the example of Brother Lawrence.

Then the glory of the Lord shall be revealed,
and all the people shall see it together.... —Isa. 40:5

NINE

Building Discerning Communities

*If we live by the truth and in love, we shall grow
completely into Christ, who is the head by whom the
whole Body is fitted and joined together....*
–Eph. 4:15-16, NJB

Have you ever tried to stay the legal distance behind
the car in front of you on a busy highway when cars
keep cutting in front of you? Trying to observe
prayerful listening in a group when no one else is
doing so produces similar frustration.[1] None of us is
capable of listening perfectly, but to the extent that we
can come to share a desire to listen, our meetings can
become places of discernment. If a group has that
desire, God will honor it and lead its members along
the path. Spiritual discernment in group deliberations
requires a communal endeavor.

We live in a culture that is not conducive to spiritual
discernment. It is difficult to maintain a discerning
attitude in our everyday life. Most of us spend a very

small percentage of our time meeting with any given church group for purposes of decision-making, so it is hard to hold on to habits of discernment cultivated there. However, these boards, committees, and assemblies are part of a larger community of faith. We very much need our various faith communities—local churches, judicatories, seminaries—to be places that nurture and reinforce the principles of discernment. If reflective sharing, reverent listening, creative exploration of Scripture, and other aspects of discernment are a part of the life of the wider church, it will be easier for us to enter into our meetings with a discerning spirit. If the church operates like the rest of society, then it will be much more difficult for us to sustain habits of discernment.

Thus, those who want to incorporate discernment into proceedings may need to become emissaries to their communities—encouraging the way of discernment and spiritual consensus broadly. Often when a group within a religious body begins practicing discernment, members find themselves introducing various elements of discernment at other church gatherings they attend. Over time—as people in the community become accustomed to using silence, reflection, non-coercive discourse, and consensus—the spirit of discernment takes hold and develops its own momentum.

Such was the case in one congregation when a group of people became involved in a discernment program.

Little by little, discernment practices spread to committees, classes, and boards. Prayerful listening and reflective silences began to filter into worship services and special events. The seeds of spiritual discernment multiplied and continue to grow.

The discerning community is a people of purpose, God's purpose.[2] There is a conscious desire to be God's servant people: loving, obedient, fruitful. The community seeks God's guidance. This may simply be a desire to be open—"Here we are, Lord. Is this a matter on which you wish to give us insight?" Or, more actively, we may ask, seek, knock—insistently and persistently. We may at times even risk being strident, relying on God's mercy should we be offensive.

When people turn to Scripture and use it to reflect on how they conduct their lives, they open up a major channel for discernment.[3] Communities prepare for discernment by making an effort to wrestle with current political, social, and personal issues through Bible study and Bible meditation. This is not because the Bible necessarily provides the answers, but because it bears witness to how God has worked through people throughout history and it has a unique power to bring us into God's presence.

It is essential that those in a group committed to discernment not hold themselves apart, but participate actively in the life of the larger community, particularly in its central worship. As the body of Christ, we all draw strength from each other. Working to become discerning bodies within the church means being open and receptive to work being done by other groups. It is important to be ready to learn from others, even if their style or emphasis differs from ours.

The fourth chapter of the Letter to the Ephesians provides a vision of Christian community. As the body of Christ, the church is an organic entity. To the extent that the many parts of the body are effectively connected to the head who is Christ, they become so knit together that they function harmoniously. The body grows in strength as it builds itself up in love. The people of the church are called to be patient, humble, gentle, charitable, and forbearing with one another—and to speak the truth in love. In such a community, discernment can flourish.

The discerning community holds in its heart a deep desire to be close to God as it considers plans, goals, finances, and strategies. The presence of its members, one to another, becomes a source of incomparable joy and strength[4] as together they become ever more securely grounded in God.

In him the whole structure is joined together and grows into a holy temple in the Lord; in whom you also are built together spiritually into a dwelling place for God.
—Eph. 2:21-22

APPENDICES
OF
PRACTICAL
SUGGESTIONS

Introduction to Appendices

Discernment is a word with a variety of applications. Even within the church, the term conveys different things to different people. When entering into a discussion about discernment, it is useful to make sure that everyone involved is talking about the same thing.

To discern means to "sort out, sift through, distinguish." Listening Hearts discernment is what St. Ignatius of Loyola called "discernment of spirits." It is distinguishing the Spirit of God from other spirits that are influencing us: the spirit of the times, the spirit of a congregation, the spirit of excelling, the spirit of giving, the spirit of efficiency—all of which may be good, but any of which can become an idol.

It sometimes helps to explain spiritual discernment with the vocabulary of call, distinguishing the voice of God from other voices that are telling us what to do— the voice of our parents etched deeply in our psyches, voices of respected teachers and mentors, voices of colleagues, voices of the media. God often speaks to us through these voices, but not everything they say is God's word for us. Spiritual discernment is a focused effort to sort out what God is saying.

One of the areas where confusion most often arises in the church is this: A person or group faces a difficult issue. They pray for God's guidance, gather relevant ideas and information, evaluate the data, apply Christian principles, make a decision, and offer closing prayers. This prayerful Christian decision-making is a kind of discernment, but it is not spiritual discernment. Spiritual discernment begins in a like manner—identifying the issue, praying for guidance, assembling information, weighing options. But it then goes on to try to discover where and how the Spirit of God has been working in the people and situation over a period of time, where God is moving at the present, and in what direction the Spirit seems to be pointing. This is a specific discipline that is contemplative in nature. It begins at the rational level, but then bids the mind descend into the heart—which in classical spirituality is at the very center of a person's being. It asks that we be centered in God and listen with all that we are. It takes place not in our heads but deep within us.

Spiritual discernment incorporates our intellects, but proceeds on the assumption that God's mind is infinitely greater than ours, God's perspective far broader than ours. It is a quest for evidence of and companionship with the Spirit. Spiritual discernment is not synonymous with what might be described as prayerful Christian decision-making. It is that and something more, something much deeper.

The appendices that follow consolidate basic considerations important to integrating spiritual discernment into meetings at which group issues are being addressed. Referring to these guidelines will make it easier for groups to implement the ideas presented in the preceding chapters.

Anyone who has practical concerns when working with the material may call the office of Listening Hearts Ministries (410-366-1851). There is no charge for such telephone consultation.

> *For who can learn the counsel of God?*
> *Or who can discern what the Lord wills?*
> *We can hardly guess at what is on earth;*
> *and what is at hand we find with labor;*
> *but who has traced out what is in the heavens?*
> *Who has learned your counsel,*
> *unless you have given wisdom*
> *and sent your holy spirit from on high?*
> *—Wis. 9:13, 16–17*

Appendix 1
Discernment Listening Guidelines

The goal of spiritual discernment is to receive God's guidance.

1. Take time to become settled in God's presence.

2. Listen to others with your entire self (senses, feelings, intuition, imagination, and rational faculties).

3. Do not interrupt.

4. Pause between speakers to absorb what has been said.

5. Do not formulate what you want to say while someone else is speaking.

6. Speak for yourself only, expressing your own thoughts and feelings, referring to your own experiences. Avoid being hypothetical. Steer away from broad generalizations.

7. Do not challenge what others say.

8. Listen to the group as a whole—to those who have not spoken aloud as well as to those who have.

9. Generally, leave space for anyone who may want to speak a first time before speaking a second time yourself.

10. Hold your desires and opinions—even your convictions—lightly.

A good way to introduce the preceding guidelines to a group for their consideration is to let a different person read aloud each guideline, pausing between each for questions and comments.

Comments on the "Discernment Listening Guidelines"

1. *Take time to become settled in God's presence.*

   People often arrive at meetings in high gear with all their wheels spinning. A period of silence gives them an opportunity to disengage from the pressures of their lives in order to become more receptive to God.

2. *Listen to others with your entire self (senses, feelings, intuition, imagination, and rational faculties).*

   Listening is not exclusively an auditory matter. People transmit their thoughts and feelings in many ways. To fully receive communication from God through fellow humans, we need to listen with all that we are.

3. *Do not interrupt.*

   Remember that these are guidelines, not hard and fast rules. Most of the time, we interrupt because we want to speak more than we want to listen. However, if someone is talking too much or straying from the subject, it may be important to interrupt for the sake of the meeting. Departure from the guidelines is appropriate if done thoughtfully, prayerfully, and for good reason.

4. *Pause between speakers to absorb what has been said.*

   A period of silence after someone has spoken gives both the speaker and the listeners a chance to assimilate what was said. Moreover, it is in those pauses that God can penetrate the group. The more profound the speaking, the longer the period of time needed to absorb it.

5. *Do not formulate what you want to say while someone else is speaking.*

   We cannot fully listen if we are thinking about what we want to say next. Notice that these guidelines are interrelated. If the group is genuinely trying to live by the guidelines, you do not have to formulate what you want to say while someone else is speaking because you feel confident that there will be spaces of silence in which you can let your thoughts come together.

   Remember that these are *discernment* listening guidelines, not meant for all times and all places. For instance, attorneys in courts of law may need to think about what they are going to say next while the opposition is speaking. Discernment, however, is not for the purpose of persuasion or prevailing. Its goal is to become aligned with God.

6. *Speak for yourself only, expressing your own thoughts and feelings, referring to your own experiences. Avoid being hypothetical. Steer away from broad generalizations.*

   In spiritual discernment we are trying to open ourselves to God's love and wisdom by being as honest and guileless as possible. The desires and fears we express should be authentic, and the information we present concrete and accurate. If we work with thoughts and feelings that people might have or events that could possibly occur, we are likely to get drawn into an intellectual exercise.

On the other hand, if specific people have made threats in relation to an issue, it is appropriate to present such information. For example, if a couple has said that they will withdraw their pledge if a proposed action is taken, good judgment may dictate that this be reported.

7. *Do not challenge what others say.*

While it may sometimes be beneficial to challenge what a person says, spiritual discernment requires the safest possible environment in which people can explore their deepest thoughts and feelings without fear of being criticized. It is normal and healthy for people to have different points of view. Rather than saying, "I disagree," those present can offer information from other sources, present alternative points of view, and recount divergent experiences. Jesus counseled us to let the weeds and wheat grow together until the harvest lest we uproot the wheat along with the weeds (Mt. 13:29, 30).

8. *Listen to the group as a whole; be attuned to those who have not spoken verbally as well as to those who have.*

If members of a group observe with all of their senses and notice each person in relation to the others, they are likely to become attuned to the needs of one another and drawn together as one.

9. *Generally, leave space for anyone who may want to speak a first time before speaking a second time yourself.*

Some people need more time than others to find the words to speak. Try to leave adequate pauses to accommodate those people. It may even be necessary to say, "Is there anyone who has not spoken who wants to do so?"

On the other hand, do not call on people or look at them in ways that could put pressure on them to speak when the Spirit may not be moving them to do so.

10. *Hold your desires and opinions—even your convictions—lightly.*

No person or group of people can comprehend God. No matter how intelligent and spiritual we are, our minds are minuscule compared with the mind of God. Our grasp of reality is always limited.

We need not discard our convictions. But it behooves us to hold them lightly as if they were resting on our open hands. In this way, we invite God to take them from us to refine them, strengthen them, or perhaps replace them.

Appendix 2
Sharing Responsibility for Practicing Discernment at Meetings

It is both the privilege and the responsibility of everyone present to help keep the group faithful to discernment guidelines in the course of the meetings. Gently making suggestions such as the following when appropriate can help the members of the group observe agreed-upon guidelines conscientiously.

- Could we take some time for silence?

- Could we take some time to become centered in God?

- Has everyone who wants to speak had a chance to do so?

- Are we truly listening to one another?

- Perhaps we could take a break and then try to refocus.

When a person is speaking too long:

- Could you wind up your remarks so that others can speak?

When a person addresses too many points:

- Could we take just one point at a time?

When someone throws a monkey wrench
into the proceedings:

- (To the individual or to the group)

  Should we stop and take this up now?

  or

  Is that something we could deal with at a later time?

When more than one person is speaking at the same time.

- Could we speak just one at a time?

Appendix 3
Checklist for Preparing an Agenda

Many groups are committed to using the "Discernment Listening Guidelines" and spiritual consensus in their meetings but find it impossible to do so because their agendas are too full. The pressure of time makes it difficult to listen to God and one another. If a group wants to incorporate spiritual discernment into its meetings, the agendas must allow ample space for listening.

1. Involve more than one person in planning agendas: "For where two or three are gathered in my name, I am there among them" (Mt. 18:20).

2. Before a planning meeting, pray for its work and prayerfully reflect on possible agenda items.

3. Upon convening a planning meeting, center in silence and prayer. Throughout the meeting, observe the "Discernment Listening Guidelines" (Appendix 1).

4. List potential agenda items.

5. Sort out matters that can be handled routinely. Determine matters that can be dealt with outside the meeting; make provisions accordingly.

6. The agenda will be less cluttered if officers and committees prepare written reports to be distributed with the agenda at least a few days prior to the meeting. Provide a place in the agenda for questions and comments on written reports.

7. Identify items that are related to one another.

8. Try to determine which item or group of related items is most important to feature at the meeting. Make that the primary agenda item.

9. When considering major items, structure the agenda so that the group can:

    • Share information and ideas.

    • Weigh options.

    • Take time to recenter in Christ.

    • Offer images and Scripture themes and passages that come to mind.

    • Share reflections on suggested images and Scripture references.

    • Look for signs of the Spirit that emerge (see Chapter 5).

    • Identify consensus.

    • Make concrete plans to act upon the discernment.

10. Integrate prayers, hymns, and silence into the agenda.

11. Identify issues excluded from the agenda that especially merit future consideration. Put them on the calendar to consider at another meeting and arrange for research or groundwork that needs to be done.

Send out the agenda and reports several days before the meeting. Ask that members of the group read them and hold the issues in prayer.

Appendix 4
Inviting Scripture and Creative Images at Meetings

O N E
Encouraging the Use of Scripture and Images

1. Make sure that members of the group know that they are invited to offer Scripture passages and creative images that come to them in the course of the meeting so that the group can reflect on them in relation to the issue at hand.

2. Keep a reflective pace so that the atmosphere permits such texts and images to come to mind.

3. Often the convener can make the time available to invite reflection when a participant shares a Scripture passage or image. If time is not available at that meeting, an opportunity to reflect on the passage or image can be made part of the agenda for the next meeting.

T W O
Setting Aside Special Time for Meditation Exercises

R A T I O N A L E
When a group faces a difficult issue, a planned Scripture meditation exercise helps to bring forth signs of the Spirit. Such meditations open new perspectives and bring the group closer to God and one another. Insights that emerge frequently provide continuing guidance as the group works on the issue.

It is important not to arbitrarily thrust a meditation exercise upon a meeting, but rather to make sure that the group is receptive to using this approach.

For Leaders Preparing a Scripture Meditation Exercise

1. Unless either a Scripture text has come out of the previous meeting or time can be provided in the meeting itself to develop Scripture references, the planning group will need to identify some relevant biblical themes or passages to use.

2. In order to choose a biblical theme or passage, be sure that the discernment question is clear and concise. Then become inwardly still.

3. In stillness, hold the issue in God. If this is difficult for you to do, it may help to hold something in your hands such as a small wooden cross, a smooth rock, or a ball of clay. Or to gaze at an object such as a cross, an icon, or a lighted candle.

4. As you sit in contemplation, a passage of Scripture may come to you. If this does not happen, quietly scan the Bible for one or more passages or images that may relate in some way. Write down the Scripture reference(s), making copies of the text(s) if feasible.

5. Consult the book *Listening Hearts Retreat Designs,* which contains a wide range of meditation exercises using such activities as writing,

drawing, walking, sculpting. Choose from among these, and simply substitute your question for the portion that asks participants to take the circumstances of their daily lives into the meditation with them. Make copies to distribute to everyone who will attend the meeting.

6. Be sure that Bibles and materials are available for each person who will be present.

A group that is well acquainted with Scripture can be asked to identify appropriate texts when it convenes for a meditation exercise. If a group is not versed in Scripture, it may be best for the planning committee to determine the texts prior to the meeting. The amount of time available is also a consideration, since developing Scripture references in the meeting requires additional time. One possibility when faced with an important issue is to schedule a special meeting explicitly for the purpose of doing a meditation exercise.

DOING A MEDITATION EXERCISE

1. If a text or image came out of the previous meeting or was developed by the planning group, present it to the group and begin the meditation exercise.

2. If texts are not already in place, have Bibles available for everyone. Ask the group to take the issue into a centering silence. After perhaps two minutes, ask that in the continuing silence participants offer aloud any images or Scripture passages that come to them.

3. Once an image, text or texts are before the group, invite the group to reflect on them and offer any thoughts or feelings that arise. If several passages have been suggested, this endeavor will probably bring a smaller number to the fore. The ones that gain energy can be used as text options for the meditation exercise. (This step will take about 30 minutes.)

4. Distribute the printed copies of the meditation exercise you prepared.

5. Read aloud the Scripture choices and go over the instructions for the exercise.

6. Ask the group to leave and return in silence. Specify a time to re-gather. (Allow about 45 minutes.)

7. When the group reconvenes, invite everyone who would like to report on the time of meditation to do so. Point out that it is a time to share reflections, not a time for discussion. Look for common threads and allow things to come together. Perhaps conclude by inviting the group to articulate the next step to be taken in relation to the issue. (Allow about 50 minutes.)

Sample Meditation Exercise
Yeast, Leaven, Culture

TO WHAT IS GOD CALLING US AS A GROUP?

The Kingdom of heaven is like yeast that a
woman took and mixed in with three measures
of flour until all of it was leavened.
—Mt. 13:33

OPTION 1: WALK

Take a prayer ring[1] to wear on your finger and place its
cross in the palm of your hand. Immerse yourself in the
question before us. Then, repeat the above Scripture text
over and over, eventually zeroing in on a few words or even
a single word. Then set out for a walk. Use the prayer ring
to keep yourself centered. Keep repeating the word or
words that you distilled from your text. Keep the Scripture
passage and our question close to your heart. Let God
touch you through the word or words. Stop to rest any time
you want. Use this hour as an opportunity for these holy
words to take root in your being. Take a watch along so that
you can get back to the group in time.

OPTION 2: DRAW

Take a number of pieces of connected computer paper and
some coloring pens with you. Take the Scripture text and
the words "yeast," "leaven," and "culture" in your heart with
you. Find a quiet comfortable place to draw. Remind yourself of our question. Then begin to express your feelings on

the first sheet of paper, using the pens. Express your feelings through movement and color and shapes. Do not concern yourself with artistic merit.

When you finish with the first sheet, stop and look at it for a while. Wait. Then either continue to draw on the same sheet or move on to draw on the second sheet. Continue in this manner, progressing from one sheet to the next. Allow enough time at the end to open up the pages and look at the series of drawings for a while.

OPTION 3: MOLD CLAY

Take clay with a plate on which to work and a chopstick for etching it. Find a comfortable place to meditate with the clay.

As you reflect on "culture" and "leaven," the Scripture text and the question, express your feelings in the clay: Press it, pound it, roll it. Shape it. Feel it. Stop to gaze at it. Try to experience this as prayer—as communication with God, as being with God. Pause often; be still that God may mold you.

The clay itself may suggest things to you. For instance, if the clay is hard to work with but then becomes more supple from the warmth of your touch, that may say something to you.

OPTION 4: WRITE

Write a hymn, story, or stream-of-consciousness passage as a way of meditating on the text and the calling of this group.

Appendix 5
Suggestions for Working Toward Consensus

Spiritual consensus is that place of unity to which the Holy Spirit has led a group. It may or may not include a decision. Christian spiritual consensus implies not merely assent, but a sense of Christ's presence among those assembled.

1. State the issue clearly; perhaps propose a solution.

2. Proceed with sensitivity to the needs of all, including their fears and insecurities.

3. Remember that, on a given issue, some people may get out ahead while others are just awakening.

4. Sense from what depth a person may be speaking and respond accordingly.

5. Be aware that a controversial situation may touch off grieving in some people and that they may need time to work through it.

6. If clarity is not coming, take comfort that now everyone is at least wrestling with the issue. Simply stating this as an observation can, on occasion, release the meeting to move forward.

7. Keep in mind that God may speak through those in the minority as well as those in the majority.

8. Always look for ways to bring together strands from differing views.

9. On occasion, it can help to check out where the group is at that moment by asking, "Where do you think we are now?"

10. Be ready to work with the pressure of deadlines, but also be open to delaying action.

11. As an issue is considered, it may become clear that it involves several components, each of which ought to be considered separately.

12. If consensus seems to be emerging, you can ask the group to either affirm or modify your understanding (for instance, "Are we in consensus that...?"), and listen to the responses for further clarity.

13. If there is apparent dissent, but a strong desire or need to take action, ask if the reservations are sufficiently strong to prevent action.

Many business matters are not controversial, and consensus may be obvious without any special effort.

Appendix 6
Practical Considerations for Meetings

ONE
Physical Setup for Meetings

1. For discernment, a circular seating arrange-
   ment is important because (a) the people can
   see one another, enabling them to listen with
   their eyes as well as their ears, and (b) a circle
   suggests community and equality, which are
   consistent with the collaborative approach of
   communal discernment.

2. A candle or meditation lamp[1] burning at the
   center of the circle can serve as a reminder of
   Christ's presence and help create a meditative
   atmosphere.

3. A quiet room, moderate temperature, and comfortable seats will make it easier for people to
   concentrate.

TWO
Breaks

Breaks are useful. If sensitively timed, they can provide
space for things to get unstuck when an impasse occurs or
time for emotions to settle when tension arises. Breaks help
prevent fatigue, restlessness, and discomfort. Yet, if rigidly
programmed, they can intrude into the work in progress to

divert energy from momentum that is developing. A short silent break can be a good option when the focus needs to be retained. Sometimes just a quick stretch helps restore people. It may help the group to be more comfortable if it is understood that anyone in the group may request a break as needed.

Appendix 7
Preparing a Group for a
Discernment Approach

Although discernment practices can be introduced to a group at regular meetings over a long period of time, a more effective way of preparing a group is to go away for a weekend or overnight retreat. An all-day workshop is another option. Whatever approach is used, each of the following suggestions will help build a solid foundation for integrating discernment into meetings.

1. To introduce the concept of discernment, arrange for everyone in the group to read *Listening Hearts: Discerning Call in Community*, at least the first five chapters.

2. Leaders and those interested in broadening their understanding of the concepts involved will want to read this book, *Grounded in God*, and books from the bibliographies of the two books.

3. Present the "Discernment Listening Guidelines" (Appendix One of this book) to the group, allowing ample time to discuss each item. After that, the group can consider adopting these guidelines as norms for the conduct of their meetings, perhaps on a trial basis for a limited number of meetings. If a particular guideline is not acceptable as presented, it can be modified or put aside for future consideration.

4. With participants taking turns, read through the ideas offered in Appendix Two, ("Sharing Responsibility for Practicing Discernment at Meetings").

5. After everyone in the group has read Chapter Six of this book ("Spiritual Consensus: A Way of Coming Together in Christ"), together go through Appendix Five ("Suggestions for Working Toward Consensus"), allowing ample time for questions and reflections.

6. Ask the members of the group to thoroughly read Chapter Five of this book, ("Catching the Signals") and Chapter Five of *Listening Hearts* ("Is It God We Are Hearing?"). Plan discussion time for this material. The *Listening Hearts Manual for Discussion Leaders* can serve as a resource for the leader(s).

7. Prepare a meditation exercise (see Appendix Four) and set aside time for the group to do a meditation exercise as a way of engaging in discernment around an issue of current importance. Build in time to (a) share reflections that come from the time of meditation, (b) develop consensus, (c) and outline a plan of action. It will be helpful if everyone in the group has read Chapter Four of this book ("Engaging the Imagination").

Appendix 8
Elements Important to Discernment Around an Issue

- Formulate the question for discernment.

- Gather information and ideas.

- Explore practical considerations.

- Evaluate the data.

- Become still and centered in God's presence.

- Let prayerful silence pervade.

- Pose evocative questions, tapping into the imagination and drawing upon Scripture.

- Provide opportunity for reflective responses.

- Look for signs of God.

- Await consensus.

- Develop plan of action.

Spiritual discernment begins with the rational and progresses toward the very center of our being. This movement from the head into the heart is crucial. Avoid flipping back and forth. First give careful attention to assembling information and ideas. Evaluate them. Then let the mind descend into the heart. Stay there, centered in God's presence, seeking signs of the Spirit.

Appendix 9
Orientation of New Members and Renewal for Continuing Groups

ONE: ORIENTATION

New members will feel more a part of the group and will be better able to participate if there is a plan to prepare them for the practice of discernment.

1. Reading the same books on discernment that the other members have read will give new people an understanding of the discernment approach as they begin their work with the group.

2. Representatives of the group can meet with new members before they attend their first meeting to introduce them to discernment guidelines and practices that have been adopted by the group. Time for questions and dialogue is essential.

3. An orientation workshop or retreat day can be planned for groups of new members.

TWO: RENEWAL

Groups that practice discernment can benefit by focusing on how they are working with discernment.

1. Time can be scheduled at the end of each meeting to reflect on how discernment is

working in the group and how to improve.
Some questions members can ask themselves:

- Are we truly listening to each other?

- Is there sufficient silence between speakers?

- Is everyone in the group who wants to speak getting the opportunity?

- Have we been looking for signs of the Spirit?

- Are we growing closer to God and one another in our meeting?

2. If the group schedules an annual retreat or workshop, all or part of the time can be devoted to reviewing discernment procedures, identifying weak areas and working to improve them, and considering steps that could be taken to further incorporate discernment into the meetings. All of this can be pursued through the use of discernment.

Some groups find it helpful to read the "Discernment Listening Guidelines" (Appendix 1) at the beginning of each meeting.

Notes

1. Compare Britain Yearly Meeting, 11.01: "...it is in meet-
    ings for church affairs that the meeting enacts its faith,"
    and 10.03: "Our shared experience of waiting for God's
    guidance in our meetings for worship and for church
    affairs, together with careful listening and gentleness of
    heart, forms the basis on which we can live out a life of
    love with and for each other and for those outside our
    community."

CHAPTER 1. SPIRITUAL DISCERNMENT:
ITS MEANING AND VALUE FOR GROUP
MEETINGS

1. St. Ignatius of Loyola, founder of the Jesuits, built on a

long history when he wrote his "Rules for the Discernment of Spirits" (Ignatius, p. 129-134) in the sixteenth century. The members of the Society of Jesus (the Jesuits) have kept the Ignatian discipline of discernment alive through the intervening years. Especially since Vatican II they have worked to apply discernment in their community decision-making (see Futrell, Orsy, Toner; also Green's "Epilogue" and Wolff, chapter 5).

Quakers have been practicing discernment for more than three centuries, and enjoy a reputation for intellectual competence and for studying issues carefully. For them, the time of discernment is one of allowing the rational to combine with the intuitive and numinous.

Jesuits, on the other hand, take more of the analytical into a process of discernment. For instance, as part of their discernment they weigh the pros and cons, and look for the spiritual and psychological roots of the opinions they have formed after they have prayed. Although this method of deliberating is not considered identical with discernment, Futrell (p. 181) writes that "Communities have found that through the use of the method of deliberation, they have finally come to realize that they have indeed fulfilled the prerequisites and that their deliberations now are authentic spiritual discernment."

2. Any thought of infallibly sensing God's direction must be rejected. As William Temple puts it, "The Christian will believe that he has an infallible authority in the Mind of Christ; but he should also know that he has no infallible means of ascertaining this in application to given circumstances. There always remains necessity for private judgment.... Infallible direction for practical action is not to be had either from Bible or Church... or individual communing with God." Temple, p. 353.

3. In the *Friends Consultation on Discernment*, p. 37, William Tabor offers one view of what it means for a group to attain the Mind of Christ: "Spiritual discernment seems to flourish best from this contemplative, reflective, non-linear state of mind which is a wide, non-judgmental almost non-attached but very alert attentiveness. Being in the Mind of Christ, however, does not mean being 'spaced out' for the analytic faculties are not suppressed; they are merely put into their rightful harmony by being surrounded and cushioned by a more vast mind which takes all things into account. Indeed, our analytical faculties are at least as sharp if not sharper in the Mind of Christ than they are at other times; the difference is that here we know that we are not just our surface mind, as we Westerners tend to assume, and the difference is that this surface mind is no longer the master, but the tool, of the more integrated person we become in the Mind of Christ."

CHAPTER 2. TOTAL LISTENING

1. Even experienced Quakers say that learning to work with silence is a lifelong endeavor for most people. Those who have not worked with silence need time and direction to introduce it into their group experience. Quakers sometimes begin working with young children by using guided meditation or other exercises to open up the inner spaces where God can be heard. Groups that have little experience with silence may need time to build up a tolerance for the length of silence. Group leaders can help by stating how long the silence will be, relieving people of the need to guess or worry.

2. The usual Quaker practice is to require members to be
    recognized by the clerk before speaking. This permits
    the clerk to create the time of silence between speakers.
    For a discussion of "wait time," see Farnham, Gill,
    McLean, and Ward, p. 125.

3. As one clerk of a Yearly Meeting put it, "Try to listen so
    carefully that you might not have to speak."

4. Compare Orsy, p. 178: "A habitually prayerful person
    will discern better in a short time than a dissipated one
    praying at length over an issue.... It is of some impor-
    tance that discernment should be made in a prayerful
    framework; it is of greater importance that those who
    discern should be prayerful persons. It follows that for
    some communities the right question is not how to dis-
    cern an issue but how to create a habit of prayer...."

CHAPTER 3. SEARCHING FOR QUESTIONS
BEFORE ANSWERS

1. Orsy, p. 168.

2. Jan Hoffman, a Quaker writer and lecturer, has offered
    an additional thought about Jesus' encounter with the
    Canaanite woman: "There is also something here about
    Jesus as a person of spiritual power allowing someone
    outside his faith community to draw out that power in
    new directions even *he* did not see at first."

CHAPTER 4. ENGAGING THE
IMAGINATION

1. Because Scripture is such an important resource for
   Christian discernment, it can be important for people
   who want to promote the practice of discernment to
   make sure that opportunities for Bible study and Bible
   meditation are available in their congregations.

2. Farnham and Miller, ed., p. 6. The author of the chant is
   unknown; words are adapted from Scripture, Ps. 46:10.

3. Chants are centering prayers put to music. A few well-
   chosen words sung over and over to a simple tune can
   help a group become quiet and allow itself to be permeated with a sense of God's presence. A group that
   develops a repertoire of chants can spontaneously
   select ones appropriate to the situation and incorporate
   them into the proceedings. The *Listening Hearts
   Songbook* contains several chants and short reflective
   hymns, some with texts in both Spanish and English.
   The Taizé community has published a book of 102 such
   meditative songs in various languages, some of which
   can be sung in harmony or as canons (*Taizé,
   Musique/Music*: J. Berthier).

4. See Meissner, p. 316: "The mystics frequently report
   experiences of divine touches, smells, and tastes to some
   extent analogous to actual sensory phenomena. It is often
   difficult to disentangle metaphoric and poetic expressions
   from sensory experience. Ignatius urged the use of the
   senses as a technique for facilitating meditation... to draw
   on the imagination to make the meditative experience

as vivid and real as possible." Also, see Ignatius, pp. 105 and 106, where he prescribes a method of prayer that draws upon the five senses. Ignatius agrees with other recognized Christian mystics that actual sensory experiences when in the mystical state are suspect (Meissner, p. 316).

Historically, Quakers have steered away from art, music, images, and the emotional, though present day Quakers believe that any of these may reveal spiritual truth.

During the latter part of the twentieth century, Carl Jung and his followers have had a profound impact on many groups of Christians, including Quakers and Ignatians. Jung brought a heightened sense of the importance of the whole and a clearer understanding of the psychological components of wholeness, which he spoke of in terms of four functions: thinking, feeling, senses, and intuition–along with other factors. He encouraged us to open ourselves to images that dwell in our inner depths– which he referred to as "the unconscious"–in order to perceive and articulate truths that we know deep within but have not been able to grasp consciously.

5.   *Listening Hearts Retreat Designs* contains several meditation exercises that individuals or groups can use to develop the potential of their imaginations for prayer.

CHAPTER 5.   CATCHING THE SIGNALS

1.   Compare Orsy, p. 157, "To fall under the spell of some trend or pressure in order to avoid a discordant note is to fall into a situation all the more dangerous because it has all the appearances of harmony, but only outwardly."

Orsy, p. 175, offers a further caution: "Also, the discerners should be aware that the judgments of the participants are not of equal value. Each moves within the limits of his own horizon, one narrow, the other broad. One remains within a tangible and material universe, the other explores the depths of the human spirit. Yet... given his stage of development, each may report joy, peace, and courage.... Even if the whole community reports peace, joy, and courage at the end of the discerning process, the common judgment or the decision reached may still be vitiated by the narrowness of the human mind and the attachments of the heart. Uniform peace does not necessarily indicate truth."

Also, compare Britain Yearly Meeting, 3.05: "It is no part of Friends' concern for truth that any should be expected to water down a strong conviction or be silent merely for the sake of easy agreement. Nevertheless we are called to honour our testimony that to every one is given a measure of the light, and that it is in the sharing of knowledge, experience and concern that the way towards unity will be found."

2. In the hymn "They Cast Their Nets," William Alexander Percy put it this way: "The peace of God, it is no peace, But strife sown in the sod." Farnham and Miller, ed., p. 40.

A similar thought was expressed in secular terms by David Grayson (pen name, Ray Stannard Baker) in *The Countryman's Year*: "Back of tranquility lies always conquered unhappiness."

3. Some of the greatest obstacles to hearing God come from within us as individuals or as a group. Cultural values that emphasize competition, efficiency, and

materialism can stand in the way of our hearing God. Prosperity and possessions can distract us from what may be the real issues before us. For example, if a church group is focused on building its endowment fund or maintaining its church building, it may avoid hearing the call to serve the poor or work on issues of justice. Similarly, the desire for security or certainty can impede our ability to hear and respond to God's call. Self-righteousness, self absorption and self-interest can prevent us from hearing God and especially from hearing God through other people. If we are focused on our needs, or on justifying our ideas or our way of doing things, we cannot hear the messages of others. Likewise, self-doubt can be a hindrance to responding to God, and perhaps even an excuse for failing to respond. It is important to examine our motives individually and corporately. For further discussion of obstacles to discernment, see Farnham, Gill, McLean, and Ward, pp. 36 & 37.

4. Orsy, p. 165.

5. For a further discussion of the signs of God's call, see Farnham, Gill, McLean, and Ward, Chapter 5, "Is It God We Are Hearing?"

CHAPTER 6. SPIRITUAL CONSENSUS: A WAY OF COMING TOGETHER IN CHRIST

1. When Jesuits seek consensus, they employ methods of deliberating that solicit and weigh the points of view of the participants in ways that analyze the roots of individual leanings in order to dissolve irrelevant conflict

and search out complementary insights that may be masked by superficial disagreements.

Quakers, on the other hand, do not expect everyone to state an opinion, nor do they measure indicators methodically. Rather, they wait upon the Spirit. They believe that the divine light is within each person and that, when gathered in focused silence, the common light will dawn through a reverent modicum of speaking. If unity does not emerge at a Quaker meeting, they refrain from moving forward on the issue at that time–although numerous subtle and subjective criteria can be applied to determine whether or not unity is declared to exist (see Sheeran, p. 71).

When Ignatians are unable to reach consensus, they are willing to resort to voting or else to delegating the decision to a committee or appointed person (Futrell, p. 184).

2. Infrequently, someone in a group cannot work with the principles of discernment. If a person persistently blocks the work of a group, an intervention may be necessary.

3. Jesuits sometimes use the terms *consensus* and *unity* interchangeably; Quakers do so less easily. Most people who practice consensus, including secular groups such as the League of Women Voters, which has used consensus for many years, generally steer away from the term *unanimous*.

4. See Britain Yearly Meeting, 3.07: "Friends should realise that a decision which is the only one for a particular meeting at a particular time may not be the one which is ultimately seen to be right. There have been many occasions in our Society when a Friend,

though maintaining her or his personal convictions,
has seen clearly that they were not in harmony with
the sense of the meeting and has with loyal grace
expressed deference to it. Out of just such a situation,
after time for further reflection, an understanding of
the Friend's insight has been reached at a later date
and has been ultimately accepted by the Society."

5. Earlier Quakers often spoke of *concord* when speaking
    of spiritual consensus; modern Quakers prefer the term
    unity.

6. Temple, p. 352.

7. Compare Quaker Resources for Learning, p. 34: "The
    unity is the underlying spirit of the meeting and it was
    that with which Fox was most concerned. Differing
    opinions can be held within one group (and differing
    actions undertaken) because the basis of unity is not
    conformity but love and concern for one another. This
    is a much deeper sort of unity, harder to achieve but
    more lasting."

CHAPTER 7.   LAUNCHING OUT

1. Listening Hearts discernment places more emphasis on
    shared responsibility than other models. For example,
    although Quakers permit participants to request more
    silence or to suggest a statement of unity, those who
    speak must be recognized by the clerk, who presides
    over the meeting and represents the corporate body.

Those who speak face the clerk and address the clerk rather than individuals or groups within the meeting. The clerk must state the unity before it is official. The clerk embodies the Meeting and thus must remain neutral on all issues being considered or else temporarily step down.

2. Orsy, p. 166. Compare Feister, p. 19, an interview with Richard Rohr in which he speaks of the need "to stay in the arena, to bear the burden of darkness."

CHAPTER 8. PLANNING MEETINGS

1. See Sheeran, p. viii: "When these local [Quaker] meetings for worship were charged with carrying out a monthly meeting for business, the mood of the meeting for worship, the openness for guidance and the close dependence and trust of each other went with it. Such a monthly meeting for business carried out the social responsibilities that were entrusted to it....

"No matter how earthy the matters to be decided might be in such a corporate exercise of decision making as the meeting for business, it was never to lose its spiritual nature. In an epistle written from Worcester prison on January 30, 1675, George Fox made clear that at their meeting for business 'Friends are not to meet like a company of people about town or parish business, neither in their men's or women's meetings, but to wait upon the Lord.'"

2. Lawrence, p. 20.

1. This analogy was offered by Edward T. Hodges at a Memorial Church (Baltimore) vestry retreat. A further implication of the analogy is that the faster we are moving, the more space we need to leave between one another.

2. Templeton, p. 139 and throughout.

3. This additional insight on the use of Scripture in group discernment has been offered by W. Bruce McPherson, Episcopal priest and trustee of Listening Hearts Ministries:
   A. Scripture is a primary way of hearing the word of God. It is the work of writers inspired by the Holy Spirit.
      • God works through the sacred story in ways that are deep and moving. The sacred story is our story, and we can find ourselves located in it differently at different times.
      • God is revealed through Scripture perhaps more clearly than in any other way except for a personal encounter with Christ, who is himself revealed in Scripture.
      • Reading Scripture slowly (in the manner of *lectio divina*) invites everyone in the group to focus seriously and intently not only on the passage and on the question for discernment, but more importantly on the presence of God.

B.   The story provides a safe context for discernment. Scripture exists independently from the issue with which the group is wrestling; it is above the fray, so to speak.

4.   Bonhoeffer, p. 19.

APPENDIX 4. INVITING SCRIPTURE AND CREATIVE IMAGES AT MEETINGS

1.   A prayer ring is a ring of beads that fits around the finger and has a small cross attached that can be held against the palm of the hand as a reminder of Christ present in us. This is made as a rosary ring and can be purchased in Catholic supply stores. Wooden ones are preferable.

APPENDIX 6. PRACTICAL CONSIDERATIONS FOR MEETINGS

1.   For information about meditation oil lamps that burn with a dancing flame, contact June Keener-Wink, 413-258-3352.

Annotated Bibliography

Berthier, J. *Taizé, Musique/Music*. Taizé-Communauté, France: Atelier et Presses de Taizé, 71250, 1995.

A collection of 102 chants of the Taizé community in various languages. The multilingual introduction includes some thoughts about singing chants.

Bonhoeffer, Dietrich. *Life Together*. New York: Harper & Row, 1954.

This book on Christian community has much of value to say to those interested in discernment for group deliberations. Specifically helpful are the discussions on the purpose and use of silence and on the ministry of listening.

Britain Yearly Meeting. *Quaker Faith and Practice*. London: The Yearly Meeting of the Religious Society of Friends (Quakers) in Britain, 1995.

This book is a gold mine for anyone interested in learning more about the discipline and heritage of the Quaker way.

Clark, Connie, ed. *Holy Meeting Ground: 20 Years of Shalem*. Washington, D.C.: Shalem Institute, 1994.

Filled with sweet humility and much wisdom on the subject of community discernment, we learn here from people who have lived into discernment and spiritual consensus these past twenty years and more, as they have practiced the presence of God.

de Waal, Esther. *A Life-Giving Way: A Commentary on the Rule of St. Benedict*. Collegeville, Minn.: Liturgical Press, 1995.

Once again, Esther de Waal has written a book full of truth and challenge—a call to discipleship, a call to come home. This commentary on St. Benedict begins with the priority: listening. Echoing St. Benedict, she bids, "Listen with the ear of the heart" (p. 5). At the point of listening, we begin our journey home to God, and find on the way the bread of life rather than the diet of empty husks we have left behind. This book will supply staying power for those engaged in the continuing work of discerning what it means to be the people of God.

Farnham, Suzanne, *et al. Listening Hearts Manual for Discussion Leaders*. Harrisburg, Pa.: Morehouse Publishing, 1993.

Farnham, Suzanne G. *Listening Hearts Retreat Designs and Meditation Exercises With Guidelines for Retreat Leaders and Covenant Groups*. Photographs by Paul Hotvedt. Harrisburg, Pa.: Morehouse Publishing, 1994.

The meditation exercises in this book can be used by individuals and groups in order to gain experience in meditating on Scripture in ways that engage the imagination to seek discernment of God's call.

Farnham, Suzanne G., Joseph P. Gill, R. Taylor McLean, and Susan M. Ward. *Listening Hearts: Discerning Call in Community*. Harrisburg, Pa.: Morehouse Publishing, 1991.

Presents the complex subject of spiritual discernment in a concise and understandable way. Integrates the wisdom and experience of Christians of many traditions. Reflective in tone.

Farnham, Suzanne G. and Louise E. Miller, ed., with illustrations by Megan Murphy. *Listening Hearts Songbook: Hymns of Discernment and Renewal*: Harrisburg, Pa.: Morehouse Publishing, 1994.

A book of fifty-two hymns from varied traditions, suitable for gatherings where music is desired as a spiritual dimension. The hymns relate to discerning God's voice through a community of faith. The music has chord notations, pen-and-ink interpretive drawings, and meditative excerpts from the book *Listening Hearts*. The songs include both contemporary and traditional hymns, chants with Spanish translations, African-American spirituals, and songs from religious communities such as Taizé in France and the Weston Priory in Vermont.

Feister, John Bookser. "An interview with Richard Rohr, O. F. M." *St. Anthony Messenger*, July 1995.

Rohr sees the discernment model of coming to truth as supplanting the church's authoritarian model.

Friends Consultation on Discernment. Richmond, Ind.: Quaker Hill Conference Center, 1985.

This brief document contains valuable teaching on the subject of communal discernment.

Futrell, John Carroll. *Communal Discernment: Reflections on Experience*. Vol. 4, no. 5 of *Studies in the Spirituality of Jesuits*. St. Louis: American Assistancy Seminar on Jesuit Spirituality, 1972.

This authoritive paper is an important resource for anyone interested in the Ignatian method of communal discernment. Concise and meaty, it includes specific suggestions.

Green, Thomas H. *Weeds among the Wheat: Where Prayer and Action Meet*. Notre Dame, Ind.: Ave Maria, 1984.

Ignatius of Loyola. *The Spiritual Exercises of St. Ignatius*. Translated by Anthony Mottola. Garden City, N.Y.: Doubleday, 1964.

This document is the original source for all writings on Ignatian discernment.

Lawrence, Brother [Nicholas Herman, 1611-91]. *The Practice of the Presence of God*. Cincinnati: Forward Movement Publications.

Meissner, W. W. *Ignatius of Loyola: the Psychology of the Saint*. New Haven and London: Yale University Press, 1992.

Written by a psychoanalyst who is also a Jesuit, this work probes the inner life of the father of Ignatian discernment.

Morley, Barry. *Beyond Consensus: Salvaging Sense of the Meeting*. Pendle Hill Pamphlet 307. Wallingford, Pa.: Pendle Hill Publications, 1993.

This booklet helps the reader understand what Quakers mean by the term *sense of the meeting* and how a community benefits by seeking a sense of the meeting as they work toward community decisions.

Noyce, Gaylord. *Church Meetings that Work*. Bethesda, Md.: An Alban Institute Publication, 1994.

A practical guide for making meetings smoother and more focused, this book offers examples and advice on working with committees or large church meetings.

Olsen, Charles M. *Transforming Church Boards into Communities of Spiritual Leaders*. Bethesda, Md.: An Alban Institute Publication, 1995.

This compilation of practical research gives examples of how church business groups operate and how they can be changed by introducing new practices that are fulfilling rather than draining. Scripture, shared stories, prayer, and discernment are among the topics discussed.

Orsy, Ladislas. *Toward a Theological Evaluation of Communal Discernment*. Vol. 5, no. 5 of *Studies in the Spirituality of Jesuits*. St. Louis: American Assistancy Seminar on Jesuit Spirituality, 1972.

This paper, written to address concerns that Jesuits face in their quest for communal discernment, is packed with insights of value to all who work to increase the practice of spiritual discernment in the corporate life of the church.

Quaker Resources for Learning. *The Search for Unity* and *Not in the Way of the World: Notes to accompany the videos on the Quaker business method*. London: Friends House.

Sheeran, Michael J. *Beyond Majority Rule: Voteless Decisions in the Religious Society of Friends*. Philadelphia: Philadelphia Yearly Meeting, 1983.

Written by a Jesuit, this book provides historical and contemporary reference points for the development of Quaker decision-making practices. The author uses case studies as well as narrative to discuss the underlying principles and belief systems involved in Quaker business meetings and leadership. Examples of the concepts of unity, meeting as worship, individual responsibility, dissent, and sense of the meeting are presented.

Temple, William. *Nature, Man, and God*. London: MacMillan and Co., 1934.

In this treasure, Temple expresses uneasiness with the application of abstract thought and principle to the matter at hand if detached "from the detail of the concrete situation" (p. 495). Even then the exercise of human judgment remains "the privilege and burden" of those involved (p. 353).

Templeton, John Marks, ed. *Evidence of Purpose*. New York: Continuum, 1994.

This collection of ten essays considers the question of whether or not the universe reflects purpose. With the exception of the editor, contributors are all scientists from fields such as astronomy, biochemistry, mathematical physics, and medicine.

Toner, Jules, J. *A Method for Communal Discernment of God's Will*. Vol. 3, no. 4 of *Studies in the Spirituality of Jesuits*. St. Louis: American Assistancy Seminar on Jesuit Spirituality, 1971.

Provides a thorough description of the underlying principles and methods for applying the Ignatian method to group discernment. The goals of individual spiritual preparation prior to communal discernment are of special interest.

Wolff, Pierre. *Discernment: The Art of Choosing Well*. Liguori, Missouri: Triumph Books, 1993.

Offers basic suggestions for implementing Ignatian discernment.

PRAYER FOR TRUST

Two part canon, sung reverently

We are afraid to put our trust in you.

Letting go of all we have is hard to do.

Give us the grace to follow where you lead

That we may embrace you both in word and deed.

Words: Suzanne Farnham and Bruce McPherson
Music: White Coral Bells
Used with Permission

Listening Hearts Series from Morehouse Publishing

Listening Hearts: Discerning Call in Community
(Revised Edition)

by Suzanne G. Farnham, Joseph P. Gill, R. Taylor McLean, and Susan M. Ward

Drawing on centuries of classic Christian literature, *Listening Hearts* provides a modern gateway to understanding age-old insights. Call, discernment, and community are explored in practical terms, aiding individuals who seek to hear and understand God's call in their lives.

The book teaches how to recognize and define God's call and how to prepare one's heart to receive that call by eliminating barriers. It also addresses how to remain faithful and attentive to God's call over a long period of time and how a community can be a source of strength and encouragement to those who respond.

Appendices contain suggestions on forming discernment groups and ministries, possible questions to raise in discerning call, as well as an informal history of Listening Hearts and the research methods used.

ISBN 0-8192-1563-5

Available from bookstores everywhere or on the Internet at www.morehousepublishing.com.

Listening Hearts: Manual for Discussion Leaders
by Suzanne G. Farnham, et. al.

This step-by-step guide tells how to prepare for and conduct discussion sessions based on the groundbreaking book, *Listening Hearts.* Inquirers, confirmation candidates, and anyone who seeks God's call through group reflection, will find the Listening Hearts experience very useful for personal growth. Listening Hearts is a unique resource that teaches how to recognize God's call; how to eliminate barriers; how to remain faithful over a long period of time; and how the strength and encouragement of our fellow "discerners" can be invaluable.

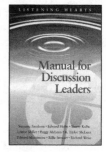

ISBN 0-8192-1608-9

Available from bookstores everywhere or on the Internet at www.morehousepublishing.com.